FEB   2016

UNDERSTANDING TAXES

LINDA CROTTA BRENNAN

Published in the United States of America by Cherry Lake Publishing
Ann Arbor, Michigan
www.cherrylakepublishing.com

Math Education: Dr. Timothy Whiteford, Associate Professor of Education at St. Michael's College
Financial Adviser: Kenneth Klooster, financial adviser at Edward Jones Investments
Reading Adviser: Marla Conn, ReadAbility, Inc.

Photo Credits: © PTstock/Shutterstock Images, cover, 1; © duncan1890/iStock Images, 5; © Drop of Light/Shutterstock Images, 6; © Tim Roberts Photography/Shutterstock Images, 9; © Monkey Business Images/Shutterstock Images, 10; © FashionStock.com/Shutterstock Images, 11; © arek_malang/Shutterstock Images, 12; © Blend Images/Shutterstock Images, 15; © Robert Kneschke/Shutterstock Images, 16; © Radu Bercan/Shutterstock Images, 19; © Pressmaster/ Shutterstock Images, 22; © Derek Hatfield/Shutterstock Images, 24; © michaeljung/Shutterstock Images, 27; © TAGSTOCK1/Shutterstock Images, 28

Library of Congress Cataloging-in-Publication Data

Brennan, Linda Crotta.
      Understanding taxes / Linda Crotta Brennan.
   pages cm. — (Real world math : personal finance)
   Includes bibliographical references and index.
   ISBN 978-1-63362-577-8 (hardcover) — ISBN 978-1-63362-757-4 (pdf) — ISBN 978-1-63362-667-6 (pbk.) —
   ISBN 978-1-63362-847-2 (ebook) 1. Taxation—United States—Juvenile literature. 2. Mathematics—Juvenile literature.
   3. Finance, Personal—Juvenile literature. I. Title.

   HJ2381.B723 2016
   336.200973—dc23   2015008967

Cherry Lake Publishing would like to acknowledge the work of
the Partnership for 21st Century Skills. Please visit www.p21.org
for more information.

Printed in the United States of America
Corporate Graphics

ABOUT THE AUTHOR

Linda Crotta Brennan has written dozens of books for young people. She has a master's degree in education and has spent her life around books, teaching and working in the library. Now she's a full-time writer who loves learning new things. She lives in Rhode Island with her husband and golden retriever. She has three grown children and a growing gaggle of grandchildren.

TABLE OF CONTENTS

CHAPTER 1

TAXES IN THE UNITED STATES

Do your parents like paying taxes? Hardly anyone does. In fact, the American Revolution (1775–1783) was sparked by a protest against taxes. On a dark night in 1773, colonists disguised as Native Americans boarded ships and dumped more than 300 chests of tea into Boston Harbor. This became known as the Boston Tea Party. Why did they do it? The colonists were protesting a tax on tea.

England had just won the Seven Years' War (1756–1763) with France, but it was a costly victory. The English felt the colonists should help pay for the soldiers who had

Colonists staged the Boston Tea Party as a protest against unfair taxes.

been sent to America to defend them. So among other things, the English taxed tea.

Before this, the colonists had been taxed only by their colonial legislatures. The English Parliament created this tea tax, and the American colonists had no representation in Parliament. The colonists felt insulted. They were paying taxes without getting any of the benefits. "No taxation without representation!" was their cry.

But even the colonists knew that taxes were necessary. After the United States won its independence, the new

Congress votes on how to use money collected as taxes.

LIFE AND CAREER SKILLS

Not paying taxes is against the law. Sometimes people refuse to pay taxes for specific reasons. Some might refuse to pay taxes that support a war. Others refuse to pay taxes that fund projects that harm the environment. In the end, they still have to pay taxes. But by protesting, they are able to draw attention to their beliefs. Do you think a person should ever break a law to support their beliefs?

REAL WORLD MATH CHALLENGE

During the Civil War, Congress passed the Revenue Act of 1861. People who earned $800 a year or more had to pay 3 percent of their **income** in taxes. Nathan Healy earned $967 in 1862.

- How much did Nathan pay in taxes?
- How much money did Nathan have left after he paid his taxes?

(Turn to page 30 for the answers)

country wrote the Constitution, which granted the **federal** government the power to collect taxes. As Americans, we vote for people to represent us in Congress, and Congress determines how our tax money is spent. This also came from the Constitution.

Taxes support three types of government: federal, state, and local. The federal government includes the president and runs the whole country. State governments run each of the 50 states. States are broken into smaller areas called counties or parishes. Local government includes the county governments and the leaders of individual cities and towns.

Canada's tax system is similar to the U.S. system. Instead of states, Canada is divided into provinces and territories.

CHAPTER 2

WHERE DOES TAX MONEY GO?

Why do we need taxes? Taxes provide us with things we use every day. What's the first thing you do when you wake up? Do you brush your teeth or take a shower? Tax dollars pay inspectors who make sure your water is pure.

Next, you probably eat breakfast. Taxes support the U.S. Food and Drug Administration, which makes sure your food and medicine are safe.

Do you attend a public school? Your school building, books, and teachers' salaries are all paid for by tax dollars.

State taxes pay for the construction of highways.

After school, do you go to the park? Maybe you head to the library. Do you ride your bike on roads? Parks, libraries, and roads are paid for by tax dollars. Taxes also help support police and fire departments. In some places, taxes pay for workers to pick up and recycle your trash.

Local taxes pay for schools, libraries, police, firefighters, and city streets. State taxes pay for state highways and bridges. They support parks and wildlife refuges and protect waterways. State governments also provide funding for education and state colleges.

Some federal tax money goes to scientists for research grants.

Federal taxes do many things. They support our military forces. They pay for interstate highways and support national parks such as Grand Canyon and Yellowstone. They help maintain historical monuments like the Statue of Liberty.

The federal government gives scientists **grants** for research. This allows scientists to do things such as study our environment, improve our use of natural resources, and search for cures for diseases. Our federal government also funds the space program, the National

Aeronautics and Space Administration (NASA).

Federal tax dollars help people in need. Imagine losing your home in a flood, hurricane, earthquake, or tornado. When a state of emergency is declared, victims can seek help from the Federal Emergency Management Agency (FEMA).

Some federal tax money goes toward disaster relief.

The government often loans college students money to pay tuition.

Do you have a brother or sister going to college? He or she may have received a grant or **loan** from the government to help pay **tuition**.

In Canada, taxes support many programs, including health care, public safety, and help for farmers.

Every office of the government receives money from **tax revenues**. Each office creates its own budget to manage how the money is spent.

Our tax money doesn't help people just in our own country. The United States also sends tax money to other nations. This foreign aid is used for a variety of things, such as disaster relief or building schools or hospitals. For example, foreign aid often helps war refugees or victims of **drought** or typhoons. Canada also gives out foreign aid. Some countries it helps include Haiti, Ethiopia, and Tanzania.

Supporting all these programs takes trillions of tax dollars. Where does all the tax money come from? Two major sources of tax revenue are sales tax and income tax.

REAL WORLD MATH CHALLENGE

Asheville has enough tax revenue to budget $34 million for education. Within the education budget, 65 percent is for instruction.

- How much money will go to instruction?
- The town has 9 elementary schools, 2 middle schools, and 1 high school. If each school receives an equal amount, how much money will each school receive for instruction?

(Turn to page 30 for the answers)

CHAPTER 3

Do the Math: Sales Tax

Have you ever bought a candy bar or a video game? Then you've probably paid sales tax. Sales tax is a percentage of an item's cost. The store collects the tax and sends it to the government. Sales tax isn't listed on the price tag, but it should be on your receipt. The percentage and the amount of sales tax are listed right above the total.

There's no national sales tax in the United States, but most states have sales tax. Internet sales aren't usually taxed, but some states have begun taxing them as well.

Sometimes there are exceptions for sales tax. Minnesota, for example, doesn't charge sales tax on clothing or food, but it does for candy. Other states charge different rates for different items.

Sales tax is charged on most items, but the laws differ among states.

If you don't remember to add the sales tax, you might not have enough money for something.

You need to consider the sales tax when deciding if you have enough money to buy something. If you have a smartphone, you can use it to calculate the tax. If you don't, you can still figure it out.

Let's say you have $75.00 to spend on a coat. You find one for $69.99. But there is a 4.5 percent sales tax. You can estimate your total purchase by rounding off. Round $69.99 up to $70.00. Round 4.5 percent up to 5 percent. Do a quick calculation of the sales tax: $0.05 \times \$70.00 = \$3.50$. Now estimate your total: $\$3.50 + \$70.00 = \$73.50$. Do you have enough to buy the coat?

Some states offer sales tax holidays. For example, Arkansas offers a holiday from sales tax on clothing and school supplies for two days in August. Buying items during a tax holiday can save you money. You can find out online if your state has a tax holiday.

Canada charges a federal sales tax, called the goods and services tax (GST). Most provinces also have a provincial sales tax (PST) on a variety of goods and services. In some provinces, the GST and PST are combined to create a harmonized sales tax (HST). That way, citizens pay one tax rate.

REAL WORLD MATH CHALLENGE

Lupita buys a box of pens for $2.29, some paper for $6.75, and a bag of chocolate for $3.98. She also buys a school sweater for $23.98. The chocolate is a grocery item, which her state has no tax on. There is an 8 percent sales tax on all other items.

- How much did Lupita pay in sales tax?
- What is the total amount of her purchase?

(Turn to page 30 for the answers)

There are other types of taxes on goods. A luxury tax once placed on things like expensive cars is now often charged to professional sports teams that spend millions of dollars to sign the best players. A sin tax is often charged on alcohol and tobacco products. The idea is that by charging a high tax on products that are harmful, people will purchase fewer of those products and be healthier.

In the United States, taxes or tariffs are charged on goods from other countries. The manufacturing of American-made goods provides jobs for the country's citizens. However, duty-free shops, which are often found in airports, allow people to buy foreign goods without paying taxes.

Sales taxes help cover the cost of many of the government services listed in the previous chapter, but not all. Where does the rest of the money come from? Here's a clue: You need an income to go shopping. And when you earn that income, you will be—you guessed it—taxed!

Duty-free shops are often found in airports.

Do the Math: Income Tax

Do you pay income tax? Probably not, but your parents probably do.

Usually, when people earn an income, automatic tax **deductions** come out of their pay all year long. Each earnings statement they get lists the type and amount of tax that is deducted. If you look at a paycheck, you will see deductions for federal income tax, state income tax, and Federal Insurance Contributions Act (FICA) tax.

The federal income tax deducted from the paycheck is used to support all the federal government programs

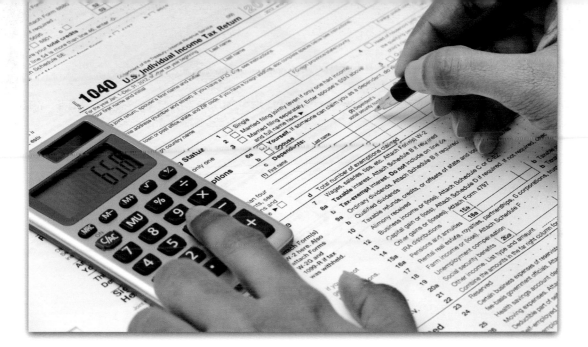

People need to file their tax returns each year.

listed in the previous chapter. Most states also charge an income tax to pay for their programs.

The FICA tax pays for Social Security benefits and Medicare. Social Security is used to help support people, such as the retired and the disabled, when they can no longer earn a salary. It also helps support **widowed** spouses and orphaned children. Medicare is a type of health insurance. It helps cover the cost of medical expenses for people over 65. It also helps seriously disabled people.

Some services help people file their taxes when things get complicated.

Employees are not the only ones who pay taxes. Employers do, too. They pay unemployment taxes. Unemployment benefits are for people who lose their jobs, to help them until they find new ones.

Canada has a similar system for collecting and distributing taxes. The Canada Revenue Agency (CRA) manages the tax system. Citizens also contribute to the Canada Pension Plan (CPP), which provides income for people who are no longer able to work. The Employment Insurance program provides income for the unemployed.

Americans who owe income tax must file tax forms with the Internal Revenue Service (IRS) once a year. The IRS determines how much federal tax you should have paid based on your gross income minus deductions, or your adjusted gross income.

Gross income is all the money you earned from January 1 to December 31 of the previous year. A deduction is money that can be subtracted from your gross income. For example, parents can take tax deductions for each of their **dependent** children. Charitable donations are also tax deductible. Tax

REAL WORLD MATH CHALLENGE

Emani has an after-school job at a fast-food restaurant. He makes $7.00 an hour. Last week, he worked 13 hours. He was surprised that 33 percent of his check was deducted for taxes.

- How much money did Emani have left?

(Turn to page 30 for the answers)

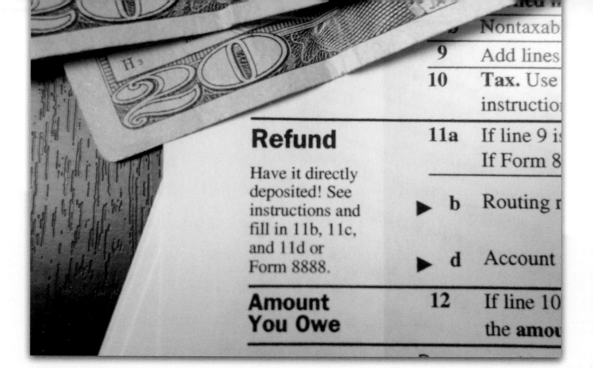

Many people receive tax refunds each year.

deductions lower the amount of your taxable income. You end up paying less in taxes.

After filing your tax form, you may discover that you paid too much tax during the year. Then you will receive a **refund** from the government. If you paid too little, you will have to pay the rest of what you owe.

States usually base their taxes on your federal adjusted gross income. But many different and complicated laws govern federal and state taxes. Some people are able to prepare their own tax forms. Often they use a computer program, such as TurboTax, to help them. Others hire tax accountants or tax attorneys to file their forms.

Most U.S. citizens must pay their federal income tax by April 15 each year. In Canada, the deadline is April 30.

Sales tax and income tax provide money that our government uses to pay for public services. There are other kinds of taxes as well. Property taxes are taxes on big items that someone owns, such as cars, boats, houses, and other buildings. In the United States, property taxes are usually charged by local governments. In Canada, the provinces charge property taxes.

People also pay taxes on **utilities** such as electricity, gas, and water, and they pay a fuel tax when they buy gasoline.

Make Your Taxes Work for You

You pay sales taxes now when you buy something. You'll pay even more taxes once you're old enough to have a job and earn an income. The money you pay goes toward all sorts of government programs. So take advantage of them!

Take your public library, for instance. Many people don't realize all the services available there. You can borrow books, of course. But did you know that many libraries offer interlibrary loans? That means you can borrow books from libraries across your area and

Tax dollars help support many of the free services offered by public libraries.

sometimes even across the country. Libraries also have magazines, CDs, and DVDs that you can borrow. Some even let you borrow things like telescopes or fishing poles. Most libraries have computer stations that provide free Internet access and wireless connections for people who bring their own laptops or tablets. All you need is a library card.

You can have a lot of fun visiting institutions supported by tax dollars. For example, admission is free at the National Zoo and the Smithsonian Museums in

For the Fourth of July, many local governments use tax dollars to put on a fireworks display.

Washington, D.C. You can also enjoy wildlife refuges, parks, and recreation areas paid for by your tax dollars.

Sometimes the government will use tax money to help fund special celebrations. Your tax dollars might support concerts, art exhibits, or theater performances. Fireworks on the Fourth of July are often paid for by tax money. The Canadian government also helps fund events such as provincial festivals.

If you have Internet access, you can take advantage of the many Web sites funded by tax dollars. Someday you

[21ST CENTURY SKILLS LIBRARY]

may go to college. When you do, you can apply for grants and loans from the government to help pay for your college expenses.

Like it or not, we have to pay taxes. Those taxes support our government and provide us with important services. Now, use your math skills to count all the ways you can make your tax dollars work for you!

LIFE AND CAREER SKILLS

In a democracy, citizens vote for the representatives who make the decisions about their taxes. In order to make wise choices, citizens must be informed. During elections, listen to what candidates have to say. When you hear about a new tax law, try to understand how it could affect you and your family. Taxes are meant to serve the common good. This means that all citizens should benefit from tax dollars. It would not be fair to pass a tax that would not help many people. When you are old enough, you will be able to vote for candidates who share your beliefs. Before then, you can support candidates through discussion with others. How else might you support a candidate?

REAL WORLD MATH CHALLENGE ANSWERS

CHAPTER ONE
Page 7
Nathan paid $29.01 in taxes.
$967.00 x 0.03 = $29.01

He had $937.99 left after taxes.
$967.00 − $29.01 = $937.99

CHAPTER TWO
Page 13
Asheville will budget $22,100,000 for instruction.
$34,000,000 x 0.65 = $22,100,000

There are 12 schools.
9 + 2 + 1 =12
Each school will receive $1,841,667 for instruction.
$22,100,000 ÷ 12 = $1,841,667

CHAPTER THREE
Page 17
Lupita spent $2.64 in sales tax.
$2.29 + $6.75 + $23.98 = $33.02
$33.02 x 0.08 = $2.64

Her total purchase was $39.64.
$33.02 + $2.64 + $3.98 = $39.64

CHAPTER FOUR
Page 23
Emani's gross income was $91.00.
$7.00 x 13 = $91.00
He paid $30.03 in taxes.
$91.00 x 0.33 = $30.03
The amount of his paycheck was $60.97.
$91.00 − $30.03 = $60.97

FIND OUT MORE

BOOKS

Bedesky, Baron. *What Are Taxes?* New York: Crabtree Publishing, 2009.

Brennan, Linda Crotta. *Taxes.* Mankato, MN: The Child's World, 2013.

Friedman, Mark. *Government: How Local, State, and Federal Government Works.* Chanhassen, MN: The Child's World, 2005.

Harper, Leslie. *Why Do We Pay Taxes?* New York: PowerKids Press, 2013.

Kowalski, Kathiann M. *Taxes.* Tarrytown, NY: Benchmark Books, 2006.

WEB SITES

BizKids—"A World Without Taxes"
http://bizkids.com/clip/de-intro
Watch a video clip about what taxes do for you.

Econedlink: Tic Tac Taxes!
www.econedlink.org/lessons/index.php?lid=370&type=student
Play games and do activities about taxes.

IRS—Understanding Taxes: Student
http://apps.irs.gov/app/understandingTaxes/student/index.jsp
Do activities about the hows and whys of taxes.

Ready—Be a Hero!
www.ready.gov/kids
Find out more about one organization that is funded by tax dollars.

TheMint: Decoding Your Paycheck
www.themint.org/kids/decoding-your-paycheck.html
Check out a sample earnings statement and see what gets deducted from a paycheck.

GLOSSARY

deductions (dih-DUK-shunz) money subtracted from a paycheck for taxes and benefits

dependent (di-PEN-duhnt) relying on another person

drought (DROUT) a long period without rain

federal (FED-ur-uhl) related to a central government or authority

grants (GRANTS) amounts of money awarded by the government for a specific purpose

income (IN-kuhm) the money that a person earns or receives, especially from working

loan (LOHN) something that is borrowed, especially money

refund (REE-fuhnd) money that has been returned

tax revenues (TAKS REV-uh-nooz) income from taxes

tuition (too-ISH-uhn) money paid to a college or private school in order for a student to study there

utilities (yoo-TIL-uh-teez) basic services such as electricity and water

widowed (WID-ohd) having lost one's husband or wife and not having remarried

INDEX